IMAGES
of America

LONG ISLAND'S
NORTH FORK

IMAGES
of America

LONG ISLAND'S
NORTH FORK

Maria Orlando Pietromonaco

ARCADIA
PUBLISHING

Published by Arcadia Publishing
Charleston, South Carolina

Library of Congress Catalog Card Number: 2003107576

For all general information contact Arcadia Publishing at:
Telephone 843-853-2070
Fax 843-853-0044
E-mail sales@arcadiapublishing.com
For customer service and orders:
Toll-Free 1-888-313-2665

Visit us on the Internet at www.arcadiapublishing.com

On the cover: Long Island Wine Country, photograph by Ralph Pugliese Jr.

CONTENTS

ACKNOWLEDGMENTS

The creation of this book would not have been possible without the contributions of many, to whom I am extremely grateful and appreciative. I would like to thank the individuals at following historical societies for sharing their knowledge and for having the patience to work with me: Norman Wamback, Mattituck-Laurel Historical Society; Geoffrey K. Fleming, Southold Historical Society; Wallace W. Broege, Suffolk County Historical Society; Allyson Reeve and Stan Rubinstein, Cutchogue Historical Society; and Amy Folk, Dan Boerum, and Bill McNaught, Oysterponds Historical Society.

Thanks also go to the photographers who provided the framework and spirit of the book: Frank K. Hartley, Hal B. Fullerman, and Ralph Pugliese Jr.

I extend my gratitude to all the families who shared their personal photograph collections.

I thank my mother for her encouragement and time; my husband, Pete, for being so supportive, showing interest, and believing in me; and the rest of my friends and family for their great enthusiasm.

INTRODUCTION

The North Fork of Long Island has always been just a bit more serene, just a little more humble, than its counterpart, the South Fork. Encompassing towns between Riverhead on the western end and Orient Point in the east, the North Fork still boasts some of the cleanest waters around, many species of thriving wildlife, a rich heritage, and countless acres of lush greenery. It remains a very special place for the residents who live here, as well as a haven for those who come to retreat.

There is no doubt that the North Fork's natural environment and geographical location helped shape its culture. Surrounded by water, abundant with gracious open spaces, and the farthest east from the big city as you can get, this particular part of Long Island lends itself to tranquility, beauty, and a more relaxed pace of life.

As you peruse the following pages, I hope you will get a sense of life how it was. You will see that many of the occupations and ways of recreation have not changed much through time. Farming, fishing, and boating are still very much alive on the North Fork.

Before the mid-1800s, the North Fork was far removed from the bustling up-island towns. In 1844, however, that began to change when the east end was linked to the urbanized west end. That year, the Long Island Rail Road completed its 95-mile track from Brooklyn to Greenport, and although it had a slow start due to a lack of popularity and necessity, it gradually gained regard after careful and rigorous marketing.

For one, the North Fork was portrayed as a vacation place—somewhere for city folks to come and bicycle, swim, and get away from it all. Secondly, the farmers greatly benefited from the fast and convenient transit of their produce, which allowed their commodity to reach consumers by the thousands.

The proximity to the Long Island Sound, Peconic Bays, and vast Atlantic Ocean has created various pastimes throughout the centuries. The mid-1800s brought about shipbuilding and repairing in the midst of the whaling boom. Around the same time, the first farmers realized that menhaden (a bunker-type fish) was a great fertilizer for their crops (information probably passed on to them by the American Indians), and the conversion of menhaden into fertilizer soon became a thriving business. Later, during Prohibition, the rumrunners kept the shipyards and repair shops extremely busy.

Marine life, such as fluke, bass, scallops, lobster, clams, and oysters, have also flourished around the North Fork for hundreds of years, and although the supply of some has been depleted as of late, many folks still take to the waters for their livelihood, as well as a source of leisure.

More recently, the wine industry has blossomed, the last 30 years bringing more than 24 vineyards to the North Fork. The climate and soil conditions seem to lend themselves to optimum grape growing, with the first 17 acres of grapes planted in 1973 by the Hargraves (actually, the first grapes were planted by the Wickham family years before), thus igniting the industry of winemaking.

The photographs in the following pages have come from many sources, including professional photographers, family collections, and historical museums and societies. I selected the photographs carefully to give an overall view of what life was really like from the latter part of the 19th century through the middle of the 20th century.

One

PORTRAITS OF
RURAL LIFE

A row of children is seated at the Greenport ferry landing *c.* 1900. (Courtesy of the Hartley Collection, Southold Historical Society.)

This photograph was taken *c.* 1910. In the decade after the turn of the century, it became acceptable for a woman to cut her hair, as you can see with the young girl on the far left. (Courtesy of the Hartley Collection, Southold Historical Society.)

Croquet players enjoy an afternoon in the sun *c.* 1900. Croquet was a popular sport in the early 1900s, especially among the North Fork's wealthy, who played on the expansive lawns of their large estates. (Courtesy of the Hartley Collection, Southold Historical Society.)

An automobile is shown at the Riverhead Fair in 1908. (Courtesy of the Suffolk County Historical Society.)

This group of farmers, the "Old Crows," got together monthly to go fishing for menhaden, also known as bunker, which they used as fertilizer for their crops. (Courtesy of the Cutchogue Historical Society.)

Captain Griffin was the captain of the ferry *Menantic*. This side-wheeled ferry ran a triangle course from Greenport to Shelter Island Heights, to Manhanset, and back to Greenport *c.* 1900. (Courtesy of the Hartley Collection, Southold Historical Society.)

A crowd gathers in front of city hall on a sandy bay-shore beach. The simplistic look of a white blouse and long, dark skirts were fashionable for leisure activities. (Courtesy of the Southold Historical Society.)

A young girl dressed in high boots and a puffy-sleeved dress stands on a porch while her kitten watches playfully *c*. 1900. (Courtesy of the Southold Historical Society.)

A yearly cleanup took place at the old cemetery in Cutchogue. (Courtesy of the Richmond family.)

A woman and girl stand in a field of flowers. Around the turn of the century, hair was piled loosely and decorated with bows and flowers. (Courtesy of the Southold Historical Society.)

Two women wait outside a hat shop somewhere in Greenport c. 1905. The corset disappeared around this time, allowing for more comfortable, straighter styles of dress. (Courtesy of the Southold Historical Society.)

Harry Conklin holds his brass instrument *c.* 1900. (Courtesy of the Southold Historical Society.)

The Greenport High School basketball team poses in their uniforms. (Courtesy of the Hartley Collection, Southold Historical Society.)

Mr. Hand and Mr. Howell, North Fork residents, seem to be discussing the catch of the day. (Courtesy of the Suffolk County Historical Society.)

MATTITUCK DAISIES

Young children play in a pasture of wild daisies in Mattituck.

POST OFFICE.

The Orient Point post office was at the home of M. Terry. Carrie Terry, the postmistress, is seated by the bicycle; Jessie Terry is on the far right. (Courtesy of the Oysterponds Historical Society.)

These folks are enjoying the sun, sand, and good company on the beaches of Orient *c.* 1920. (Courtesy of the Oysterponds Historical Society.)

The 1920s marked a turning point for women's bathing suit fashions. A variation of the men's swimsuit, these one-piece bathing outfits allowed for freedom in the water. (Courtesy of the Oysterponds Historical Society.)

Sun seekers on the North Fork c. 1920 did not always wear swim gear. Trousers for women came that decade, and it was finally realized that fashions could be functional. (Courtesy of the Oysterponds Historical Society.)

At Laurel Lake, Mattituck, L. I.

Three gents and three young boys prepare to do some fishing on Laurel Lake in Mattituck.

The Cove towards Klein's.   MATTITUCK, L. I.

Three women, sufficiently covered from the sun in the era's fine fashions, savor a day on Mattituck's Cove *c.* 1890.

Standing at the monument with the first Farmall tractor are, from left to right, Russell Tabor, Kenneth Tabor, Herman Stanley Duvall, Frederick Tabor (father of the mentioned Tabors), and Edwin Hadden King. All of these men were Orient farmers. The Tabor House is in the background of this 1940 photograph. (Courtesy of the Oysterponds Historical Society.)

Skaters pose on East Marion Lake on Christmas Day 1897. (Courtesy of the Oysterponds Historical Society.)

This is the home of Charles Sidney Tuthill in South Jamesport. The building on the right and the team and wagon in the driveway were used by Charles and his brother George Henry Tuthill in their undertaking establishment. (Courtesy of the Suffolk County Historical Society.)

One fisherman, one rower, and one supervisor are on Laurel Lake in Mattituck.

A man and a boy stand with a horse near the Union School. (Courtesy of the Hartley Collection, Southold Historical Society.)

Children pose on Westphalia Road in Mattituck.

Elizabeth and Joseph Krupski are pictured with three of their children: Julius, Frances, and Helen. The Krupskis are one the oldest farming families on the North Fork.

26

The Girl Pioneers of America march in a parade on July 7, 1913. (Courtesy of the Suffolk County Historical Society.)

Eight tennis players gather at the net for a photograph. (Courtesy of the Hartley Collection, Southold Historical Society.)

This parade is on First Street in Greenport. The view looks west toward the Sterling Food Market. (Courtesy of the Hartley Collection, Southold Historical Society.)

A mother and her children wait on a dock at Shady Point along Mattituck Creek in Mattituck.

Two brothers show off their kill after a day of duck hunting.

Children line up in front of the Demonstration Farm at the Riverhead Fair in 1916. (Courtesy of the Suffolk County Historical Society.)

29

People gather at the Civil War monument in Orient on May 30, 1913. (Courtesy of the Oysterponds Historical Society.)

These men, women, and a child are posing in front of the United States Hotel. Later, this was the location of Victoria's Bowling Alley on Peconic Avenue, owned by J.M. Burgess. It was known as the Riverhead Cottage.

Railroad officials gather at the Riverhead Fair in 1908. (Courtesy of the Suffolk County Historical Society.)

Children stand on the shore of Orient. They are, from left to right, unidentified, unidentified, Donald Rackett, Hilda Rackett (now Hilda Wilcox), and Eva Tuthill (now Eva King). (Courtesy of the Oysterponds Historical Society.)

Pictured here are "the Picksies," an Orient girls' group organized by H.F. Knobloch *c.* 1928. From left to right are Martha Terry, Florence Adams, Mary Anna Vail Parks Muir, Mrs. H.F. Knobloch, Lillian Vail Hallock, Mae Ryder Conklin, Cathryn Young, Blanche Latham, Elizabeth Beebe Vail, Sarah Adams Wiggs, Ruth Vail Luce, unidentified, and Helen McClymont Robertson. (Courtesy of the Oysterponds Historical Society.)

Three generations of women and children pose on a porch in Southold *c*. 1898. (Courtesy of the Hartley Collection, Southold Historical Society.)

This is another shot of the previously mentioned Old Crows, a club of farmers-turned-fishermen. (Courtesy of the Hartley Collection, Southold Historical Society.)

The St. Isadore Society is shown in front of the St. Isadore Church in Riverhead in 1895. Polish immigrants erected the church in an attempt to keep their heritage alive. St. Isadore is the patron saint of farmers. (Courtesy of the Suffolk County Historical Society.)

This is the A.F. Sammis automobile exhibit at the Riverhead Fair in 1908. (Courtesy of the Suffolk County Historical Society.)

The Riverhead Brass Band is shown in August 1910. From left to right are the following: (front row) Clarence Dugan, Forrest Downs, Carl Hallett Jr., Fred Hallett, Harry Moore, Archibald Hallett, and Carl LeValley; (back row) George LeHommedieu, Fred Hill, Hans Walty, Sam Barber Jr., Nathan Corwin, Paul Brown (child), unidentified (behind Brown), Lewis Young, Cornelius Mazurie, Ed Carter (behind Mazurie), Burt LeHommedieu, Howard Lane, Matthias N. Amman, and John Madden. (Courtesy of the Suffolk County Historical Society.)

This is the firemen's parade in Riverhead in June 1937. (Courtesy of the Suffolk County Historical Society.)

Orient captains who skippered vessels between 1880 and 1900 meet in this photograph. Those in attendance include Mr. Corwin, David Edwards, Bill Terry, Marcus Brown, Henry Rackett, J.H. Young, Lester Terry, and G. Rackett. (Courtesy of the Oysterponds Historical Society.)

Only some of these students at the Orient School are identified: Seward King (front row, second from the left), Maude Douglas Latham (back row, third from the left), Iva Glover Luce (back row, fourth from the left), Florence Adams Kobler (back row, sixth from the left). (Courtesy of the Oysterponds Historical Society.)

The Orient Players are shown here in 1885. (Courtesy of the Oysterponds Historical Society.)

The Pequash Recreation Club, a private men's social club, gathered monthly at a house on Peconic Bay. (Courtesy of the Cutchogue Historical Society.)

This family portrait was taken c. 1902. (Courtesy of the Hartley Collection, Southold Historical Society.)

A group of elementary school students is gathered in Jamesport in the late 19th century. From left to right are the following: (front row) Stella Homan, Alice Luce, Willard Albin, Roy Griffing, G. Benjamin, Mable Petty, Elmer Hallock, and Brentwood Albertson; (middle row) Harry Hawkins, unidentified, Laura Tuthill, Mary Cornwell, Mary Ethel Benjamin, Minnie Hallock, Jennie Jones, and Nellie Hawkins; (back row) Lena Woodhull, Everett Petty, Pauline Albertson, Everett Frederick, Ben Griffing, Iva Wells, Minnie Jones, and Maud Albertson. (Courtesy of the Suffolk County Historical Society.)

Louise Johnson Hallock is shown in her science class at Mattituck High School during the 1912–1913 school year. (Courtesy of the Mattituck Historical Society.)

Bicycling became extremely popular on the North Fork in the early 1900s, especially for women. Unfortunately, sport clothes were unavailable and unacceptable, and women found it difficult to ride in the long skirts and layered undergarments they were required to wear. (Courtesy of the Hartley Collection, Southold Historical Society.)

These six women are seated at what seems to be a birthday celebration. From left to right are ? Cox, Kate Fleet, Sadie Tuthill, Annie Gould, Annie Beebe, and Madilyn Bartow. (Courtesy of the Cutchogue Historical Society.)

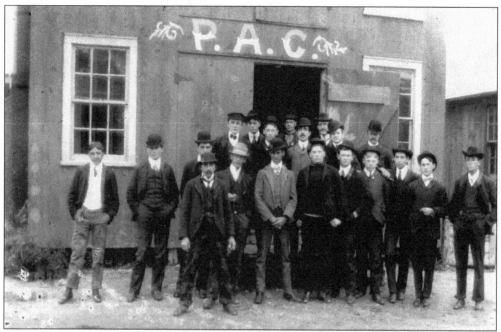

The Portsonian Athletic Club is pictured outside club headquarters. (Courtesy of the Hartley Collection, Southold Historical Society.)

The Mattituck Marching Band is pictured c. 1900. From left to right are the following: (front row) Prof. George B. Reeve, Howard Terry, ? Wallace, ? Tuthill, George Terry, Willis Tuthill, Jim Reeve, Otto Hallock, and Lucius Young; (back row) E.B. Knipe, Oscar Robinson, Harvey Duryee, Gene Robinson, Herbert M. Reeve, Will Duryee, Wickham Reeve, Harry Lupton, and M.P. Goff. (Courtesy of the Mattituck-Laurel Historical Society.)

The members of this *c*. 1885 Oregon baseball team are, from left to right, as follows: (front row) ? Shalvey, Garret Duryee, William V. Duryee, and Philip Duryee; (back row) William B. Reeve, Ernest Hamilton, ? Tuthill, Jim Lindsay, and George Terry. (Courtesy of the Mattituck-Laurel Historical Society.)

These sixth- and seventh-grade students pose in front of Mattituck School in 1913. The teacher, in the back, is Miss Stanley. The students are, from left to right, as follows: (front row) Matilda Sonntag, Mary Gallagher, Adelaide Salterly, Hazel B. Tuthill, Edna Jackson, Hope Duryee, Elizabeth Cooper, Dorothy Burus, Kathyrine Baylis, Hazel B. Tuthill, and Amy Smith; (back row) Luther Cox, John Barker, John Duryee, Irving Comisky, George McMillan, John Mahoney, Robert Wasson, Frank Cantellmi, Sidney Tuthill, Channing Downs, George Eldred, and Benedict Linsey. (Courtesy of the Mattituck-Laurel Historical Society.)

The New Egypt School, in West Mattituck, is pictured in 1899. It is now the site of the Mattituck-Laurel Historical Society and Museums. The original school was built in 1846. Some students in the picture represent the Reeve, Robinson, Cooper, Aldrich, and Howell families. (Courtesy of the Mattituck-Laurel Historical Society.)

A family gathers in the front yard in Greenport *c*. 1897. (Courtesy of the Hartley Collection, Southold Historical Society.)

UNIVERSITY OF THE STATE OF NEW YORK.

Preliminary Academic Examination.

BY THE REGENTS OF THE UNIVERSITY OF THE STATE OF NEW YORK:

WHEREAS, the COMMITTEE of EXAMINATION and the PRINCIPAL of

Bridge Hampton Lit & Com'l INSTITUTE

have certified to the REGENTS OF THE UNIVERSITY that at an Examination held by the appointment of the said REGENTS, February 28th and March 1st, 1878,

Jeremiah G Tuthill

was found to have made the attainments required by their Ordinance, for admission to the ACADEMIC CLASS,

AND WHEREAS, his papers, on review at this office, have been found satisfactory,

THEREFORE, he has been duly registered by the said REGENTS in their office as an

ACADEMIC SCHOLAR,

and all Academies and Institutions of learning, subject to their visitation, are authorized to receive him as such, without further examination.

IN WITNESS WHEREOF, the said REGENTS have caused the names of their Chancellor and Secretary to be hereto affixed, at the City of Albany, this tenth day of April, one thousand eight hundred and seventy-eight.

E. C. Benedict
Chancellor of the University.

S. B. Woolworth,
Secretary.

Jeremiah Tuthill's regents certificate was awarded from the Bridgehampton Literary and Commercial Institute in 1878. Tuthill, the son of Jeremiah Goldsmith Tuthill and Hanna Rosetta Howell, was born in 1861 and was one of eight children. There are thousands of Tuthills on the Tuthill family tree on the North Fork alone, descendants of Henry Tuthill Sr., from England. Henry Tuthill Jr. first arrived in Southold in 1644. (Courtesy of the Cutchogue Historical Society.)

Two

BUSINESS AS USUAL

W.E. Shipman's blacksmith shop is pictured in a view looking north. The village hall is on the right. (Courtesy of the Hartley Collection, Southold Historical Society.)

This is the home of the Dettners on Roanoke Avenue in Riverhead. Henry Dettner and his dog Nip are on the right. (Courtesy of the Suffolk County Historical Society.)

J.B. Young's grocery and meat store was later the home of P. Caffey. (Courtesy of the Oysterponds Historical Society.)

The Riverhead Fire Company is pictured in 1911. (Courtesy of the Suffolk County Historical Society.)

George T. Billard and Ellis F. Billard are shown in Cutchogue at Billard's Market in the early 1930s. (Courtesy of the Cutchogue Historical Society.)

A construction crew revamps a storefront on Front Street in Greenport. (Courtesy of the Hartley Collection, Southold Historical Society.)

A horse-drawn delivery wagon is shown in front of the John F. Fish grocery store. (Courtesy of the Hartley Collection, Southold Historical Society.)

This *c.* 1900 image shows store owner Mr. Woodhull (left) and watchmaker Nathaniel Peterson. The store was situated on the south side of East Main Street in Riverhead. (Courtesy of the Suffolk County Historical Society.)

Four men stand outside the home of the Suffolk Weekly Times, the newspaper that has served Southold, Greenport, and Shelter Island since 1857. (Courtesy of the Hartley Collection, Southold Historical Society.)

This is D.C. Petty's beer wagon. (Courtesy of the Hartley Collection, Southold Historical Society.)

Employees stand in front of the Wells Coal and Wood office, near the docks in Greenport. Coal was a big business at the turn of the century, when ships converted to steam. It was also used to heat homes. (Courtesy of the Hartley Collection, Southold Historical Society.)

Louis Young's horse-drawn coal cart is shown here in Greenport, where coal was brought in on ships from New England. (Courtesy of the Hartley Collection, Southold Historical Society.)

The Orient post office is now a private residence. (Courtesy of the Oysterponds Historical Society.)

This garage was owned by Alfred Luce. It was blown apart in the Hurricane of 1938. (Courtesy of the Oysterponds Historical Society.)

Cicero B. King owned this store. (Courtesy of the Oysterponds Historical Society.)

People work at the icehouses in Orient. The clean waters of the coves and millponds made for excellent ice making. The blocks of ice were transported from several locations on the east end, westward to the city. (Courtesy of the Oysterponds Historical Society.)

Fred and Mabel Richmond are shown in their store in the late 1920s or early 1930s. The store was originally built in the 1700s and owned by a member of the Tuthill family. Rumor has it that Albert Einstein frequented the establishment the one summer he spent on the North Fork.

Located on Main Road in Peconic, it is now known as the Down Home Store. (Courtesy of the Richmond family.)

A crowd gathers in front of the L.V. Beebe store, where you could buy anything from meat and groceries to lumber and real estate. (Courtesy of the Oysterponds Historical Society.)

Frank C. Cooper is in front of his shoe store on East Main Street in Riverhead in August 1916. (Courtesy of the Suffolk County Historical Society.)

The Rocky Point Life Saving Station and crew are pictured in East Marion. (Courtesy of the Oysterponds Historical Society.)

The Rocky Point crew would rescue ships in distress along the eastern Long Island Sound. This building is now a private summer residence. (Courtesy of the Oysterponds Historical Society.)

Elisha Rackett and Jim Dewey are shown in front of the Young and Rackett store. (Courtesy of the Oysterponds Historical Society.)

Five men pose in the C.B. Wiggins general store. (Courtesy of the Hartley Collection, Southold Historical Society.)

This general store is unidentified.

Ice is pushed out through the sluiceway on the west side of East Marion Lake. (Courtesy of the Oysterponds Historical Society.)

C. Ambrose King and his dog Coach are in front of John Kokendaffer's home on King Street. The King Brothers operated out of the former J.B. Young store on the west side of Village Lane. (Courtesy of the Oysterponds Historical Society.)

Fred Richmond is at the gas pumps in front of the Richmond store. (Courtesy of the Richmond family.)

Three

TOWN AND COUNTRY

This photograph shows the H.E. Young Livery Stable. Travelers could rent stalls at livery stables to keep their horses while they were in town. (Courtesy of the Hartley Collection, Southold Historical Society.)

This view looks north onto Love Lane in Mattituck from Main Road, before electricity. (Courtesy of the Mattituck-Laurel Historical Society.)

This is the business center in Mattituck. The barbershop still exists today. (Courtesy of the Cutchogue Historical Society.)

Pictured after a storm, these wooden fences have protected the road in Orient c. 1900. (Courtesy of the Oysterponds Historical Society.)

This is the East Marion Baptist Church before alterations were made. (Courtesy of the Oysterponds Historical Society.)

Ye Clarke House is pictured here in Greenport. Capt. John Clark had this inn built for him by Capt. Caleb Dyer of Orient. It opened in 1831 and closed in 1927. Famous guests included John Quincy Adams, Walt Whitman, and James Fennimore Cooper. (Courtesy of the Cutchogue Historical Society.)

Main Street in Cutchogue featured the Cutchogue Pharmacy, which sold ice cream, soft drinks, and medical drugs. (Courtesy of the Cutchogue Historical Society.)

The Hotel Dennis, in Greenport, is pictured here c. 1910. It was formerly the Griffing House and later became the Greenport House. (Courtesy of the Cutchogue Historical Society.)

The Old Red Mill, in Riverhead, is pictured here. (Courtesy of the Suffolk County Historical Society.)

This is the Mattituck House, located in Mattituck on the corner of Love Lane.

The Hallett family started the Hallett Mill in Riverhead in 1696. It is the oldest flour mill in the country. In the mid-1800s, Charles Hallett ran a moulding and planing mill. (Courtesy of the Suffolk County Historical Society.)

This is another view of the Hallett Mill in Riverhead (see the previous page).

Sylvester Woodhull's house is pictured in 1888 with the Old Red Mill and a portion of Peconic Avenue. (Courtesy of the Suffolk County Historical Society.)

The water tower in Grangabel Park, in Riverhead, is shown in the early 1900s. (Courtesy of the Suffolk County Historical Society.)

A funeral procession is pictured *c*. 1905. (Courtesy of the Hartley Collection, Southold Historical Society.)

When this photograph was taken, the Greenport Opera House was showing *The Mail is Open* at 1:30 p.m. The building was located at the corner of Bay and Main. The site is now a parking lot. (Courtesy of the Hartley Collection, Southold Historical Society.)

This is the C.H. Fischer Market, located in Mattituck at the southeast corner of Pike Street and Love Lane. (Courtesy of the Hartley Collection, Southold Historical Society.)

Front Street in Greenport is shown in this view looking west. A livery wagon is in the center. (Courtesy of the Hartley Collection, Southold Historical Society.)

An aerial view of Greenport features R.J. Claudio's restaurant, which was established in 1870 by Manuel Claudio, a whaler from Portugal. Still owned by the Claudio family, the establishment celebrated its 133rd anniversary in 2003. (Courtesy of the Hartley Collection, Southold Historical Society.)

J.W. Ketcham's Boat Shop is pictured here. (Courtesy of the Hartley Collection, Southold Historical Society.)

This is a closer view of the R.J. Claudio building in Greenport. (Courtesy of the Hartley Collection, Southold Historical Society.)

A view of Main Street in Riverhead looks west from Peconic Avenue. Judge T.M. Griffing's house is in the center. (Courtesy of the Suffolk County Historical Society.)

The village in Riverhead is shown in a view looking east on Main Street in July 1938. (Courtesy of the Suffolk County Historical Society.)

Krupski's Pumpkin Farm, on Main Road in Peconic, is one of the largest on the North Fork. (See the family photograph on page 26.) (Courtesy of the Cutchogue Historical Society.)

The Glenwood Lodge, on Route 25 in Mattituck, is pictured here. Built in 1860, it was sold in 1892 and became the Hotel Glenwood. It was sold again in 1919 and renamed the Glenwood Lodge. During Prohibition, it had a fancy speakeasy in the basement. It is a lawyer's office today. (Courtesy of the Cutchogue Historical Society.)

This photograph shows Macadam Road and Griffing Avenue in Riverhead. (Courtesy of the Suffolk County Historical Society.)

This is a view of the waterfront from the dock in Orient. (Courtesy of the Orient Historical Society.)

This image offers a bird's-eye view of Mattituck.

A fruit and stationery store in Mattituck is shown here.

This view looks west on Main Street in Riverhead in July 1945. (Courtesy of the Suffolk County Historical Society.)

MAIN STREET, JAMESPORT, LONG ISLAND, N.Y.

This is the traffic light on Main Street in Jamesport. (Courtesy of the Cutchogue Historical Society.)

Eastern L. I. Hospital, Greenport, L. I.

Eastern Long Island Hospital, in Greenport, is shown in this image. Built by Capt. John Monsell in 1856 as a residence, it was later donated and became a hospital. (Courtesy of the Cutchogue Historical Society.)

A 8142 Opera House, Greenport, L. I.

This postcard of the Greenport Opera House was mailed in 1907. (Courtesy of the Cutchogue Historical Society.)

Peconic Avenue is pictured on July 4, 1938. (Courtesy of the Suffolk Courtesy Historical Society.)

This is a 1917 photograph of the business district in Riverhead. (Courtesy of the Suffolk County Historical Society.)

A view of Main Street in Greenport looks toward the wharf in 1912. (Courtesy of the Cutchogue Historical Society.)

The Methodist Campgrounds in Jamesport were started in 1853 by a group of Methodists who set up tents in a grove of tall oak trees in Jamesport. They returned every summer to enjoy the tranquility of the location and later built Victorian cottages on the site, which remain today. (Courtesy of the Cutchogue Historical Society.)

The icehouse on Rabbit Lane in East Marion is pictured c. 1908. (Courtesy of the Oysterponds Historical Society.)

The "Old House," one of the oldest houses in New York, was built in 1649 in Southold by John

Budd. It was moved in 1660 to its present location in Cutchogue. (Courtesy of Ralph Pugliese Jr.)

This view of Main Street, from Front Street in Greenport, features Corwin's Drug Store. (Courtesy of the Cutchogue Historical Society.)

Billard's Old Cider Mill was purchased and moved to the Wickham Farm. It is still in use today. (Courtesy of the Cutchogue Historical Society.)

This is the Griffing Park entrance on the Peconic River in Riverhead. (Courtesy of the Suffolk County Historical Society.)

This postcard, sent in 1913, shows the Ulmer Block in Greenport. (Courtesy of the Cutchogue Historical Society.)

Pictured here is the sign in front of the Orient Point Inn. (Courtesy of the Oysterponds Historical Society.)

Four

SEAFARING FOLK

The Greenport Basin and Construction Company launches *Mascot*. (Courtesy of the Hartley Collection, Southold Historical Society.)

The *Manhanset* was captained by Jim out of Greenport. The vessel was named after an American Indian tribe on Shelter Island. (Courtesy of the Cutchogue Historical Society.)

Iceboating was a favorite pastime in the winter months. This photograph was taken on a frozen cove somewhere in Greenport. (Courtesy of the Hartley Collection, Southold Historical Society.)

This is another iceboating scene.

Two men and a woman are possibly trying to figure out exactly how to launch their rowboat. (Courtesy of the Hartley Collection, Southold Historical Society.)

The shipwrecked schooner *Escort* is pictured in 1898, west of the Peconic Inlet. Standing on the beach are, from left to right, Lester Albertson, Corey Albertson, George Bladworth, and John Howell (Bob Pettit's great-uncle). (Courtesy of the Hartley Collection, Southold Historical Society.)

An "Aztec" diver is at work for a construction company in Greenport. (Courtesy of the Hartley Collection, Southold Historical Society.)

This is the armed forces Home Guard in 1898. John Geehreng is on board *Kelpie*. (Courtesy of the Hartley Collection, Southold Historical Society.)

Swimmers enjoy the waters off Orient. (Courtesy of the Oysterponds Historical Society.)

These boaters are on Marion Lake in East Marion. (Courtesy of the Oysterponds Historical Society.)

Mr. Hand, his pooch, and a pal relish in a day of fishing and puffing. (Courtesy of the Suffolk County Historical Society.)

The steamer *Shinnecock* is shown on Gardiner's Bay off Shelter Island. (Courtesy of the Suffolk County Historical Society.)

A nice catch of sea bass is shown aboard the *Black Eagle*. (Courtesy of the Oysterponds Historical Society.)

Capt. John Fournier was a fluke fisherman in Gardiner's Bay in East Marion. He is shown here in 1902. (Courtesy of the Suffolk County Historical Society.)

Eighteen people swim here in the Gull Pond c. 1910. (Courtesy of the Hartley Collection, Southold Historical Society.)

Two men are geared up for duck hunting, a popular sport on the North Fork.

The *Black Eagle* is shown at the Village Wharf. (Courtesy of the Oysterponds Historical Society.)

A family enjoys a picnic on a Long Island Sound beach in Southold *c.* 1900. (Courtesy of the
Hartley Collection, Southold Historical Society.)

The Greenport Basin and Construction Company launches *Sandsucker*. (Courtesy of the Southold Historical Society.)

These swimmers are in a bay on a boating platform in Shelter Island Heights. (Courtesy of the Southold Historical Society.)

Girl Pioneers are shown on the Peconic River in Riverhead in 1913. From left to right are Louise Wells, Marion Terry, Olive Tuthill, Frances Barnes, Edith Whitney, Jessie Fordham, Margaretta Carleton, and Grace Corwin (pushing the boat). (Courtesy of the Suffolk County Historical Society.)

A double-decker Greenport ferry is pictured at the new Shelter Island landing c. 1910. (Courtesy of the Cutchogue Historical Society.)

A steam yacht is shown in Greenport in 1899. (Courtesy of the Suffolk County Historical Society.)

Four men enjoy a day on the water in a rowboat somewhere in Greenport. (Courtesy of the Hartley Collection, Southold Historical Society.)

A day of sailing is enjoyed in Orient. (Courtesy of the Oysterponds Historical Society.)

A group of women is shown in a catboat in August 1904. (Courtesy of the Hartley Collection, Southold Historical Society.)

Five

WHEN DISASTER STRIKES

A major hurricane hit the Northeast on September 21, 1938. Extensive damage was done on
the North Fork.

The hurricane took more than 500 lives in all. Many folks on the North Fork have their own stories to tell.

This is the aftermath on Main Road through Aquebogue.

106

Thousands of trees were lost. The highest wind velocity recorded was 183 miles per hour in Milton, Massachusetts.

This car avoided being crushed by only inches. North Fork residents had no warning of the hurricane. In fact, many had never heard of a hurricane.

An incredible image depicts of a row of downed trees on Main Road in Southold.

The 1938 hurricane destroyed 16,740 structures, including one of Tuthill's storage warehouses.

There was a lot to be done in the weeks after the storm. The cleanup was enormous.

These trees in Cutchogue did not stand a chance and were right in the path of harm's way.

Due to a tremendous number of downed power lines, people on the North Fork went without phone service and electricity for days.

You can see the hurricane's rage by the size of the trees it took to the ground. By the time it reached the North Fork, it was a Category 3, with winds up to 130 miles per hour.

The streets were a mess after the fallen branches and leaves wreaked havoc on the roads.

Roads were hard to pass and stayed that way for a while.

North Fork residents survey the hurricane's damage.

It is hard to tell whether this house is sinking or if the roof blew off into a field.

This is the famous train wreck of the *Cannon Ball Express* out of New York City into Calverton on August 13, 1926. (Courtesy of the Mattituck-Laurel Historical Society.)

The train slammed into a pickle factory, killing several passengers, including the engineer, who drowned in a vat of pickles. (Courtesy of the Mattituck-Laurel Historical Society.)

A fire broke out at the home of Dr. Miles. (Courtesy of the Hartley Collection, Southold Historical Society.)

A fire rages on Main Street in Riverhead. (Courtesy of the Suffolk County Historical Society.)

On November 17, 1935, Peconic Avenue in Riverhead flooded. It flooded again in 1950 and 1953. (Courtesy of the Suffolk County Historical Society.)

Six

THE WORLD OF WINE

The sunflowers at Pindar Vineyards bloom in midsummer. (Courtesy of Ralph Pugliese Jr.)

The Braud grape harvester and gondola harvest grapes in early fall. (Courtesy of Ralph Pugliese Jr.)

Long Island Wine Country has more than 3,000 acres of grapes and 27 wineries, most of them on the North Fork.

Kip Bedell, a winemaker, founded Bedell Cellars. Bedell Cellars opened its tasting room in 1985, and Bedell won his first gold medal soon after for his 1986 Reserve Chardonnay.

The North Fork produces many award-winning red wines, including Merlot, Cabernet Sauvignon, Cabernet Franc, and Syrah. (Courtesy of Ralph Pugliese Jr.)

Jamesport Vineyards planted their first vines in 1981, and they are among the North Fork's oldest. (Courtesy of Ralph Pugliese Jr.)

Pindar's Harvest Festival draws thousands every October.

Mark Friszolowski is a winemaker at Pindar Vineyards. He makes several award-winning wines, including the Pindar's Mythology, a Meritage red.

Peggy Lauber, co-founder of Corey Creek Vineyards, hand-harvests Pinot Noir in 1998.

Laurel Lake Vineyards was established in 1994. Claudio Zamorano is the winemaker. (Courtesy of Ralph Pugliese Jr.)

Dr. Herodotus Damianos, also known as Dr. Dan, is pictured at a social gathering with his friend Ralph Pugliese Sr. of Pugliese Vineyards.

Dr. Dan is shown with his sons, Jason and Pindar. Jason is the winemaker at Duckwalk Vineyards, located in Southampton. Pindar also studies winemaking.

The Krupski potato barn is now the home of Pindar's tasting room and winery.

Joann Orlando of Pindar Vineyards stands next to a Gregorie grape harvester, an enormous machine used in many vineyards to collect grapes in the fall.

Russel Hearn, a winemaker at Pellegrini Vineyards, is shown in 1997.

124

Bob and Joyce Pellegrini established Pellegrini Vineyards in 1991.

Chardonnay grapes wait to be pressed. (Courtesy of Ralph Pugliese Jr.)

This is the retail tasting room at Corey Creek Vineyards.

Chardonnay grapes are harvested at Corey Creek.

126

Bob Palmer is the founder and owner of Palmer Vineyards, and Tom Drozd is Palmer's winemaker.

Corey Creek Rose is bottled at Pellegrini Vineyards.

Scott Osborne retrieves a barrel sample for Dr. Dan at Pindar Vineyards.

Merlot juice pours out of a wine press. (Courtesy of Ralph Pugliese Jr.)

Visit us at
arcadiapublishing.com